# Diana

## The Illustrated Biography

# Diana
# The Illustrated Biography

ALISON GAUNTLETT

Photographs by

**Daily Mail**

Trans
Atlantic
Press

Published by Transatlantic Press
First published in 2008

Transatlantic Press
38 Copthorne Road
Croxley Green, Hertfordshire
WD3 4AQ, UK

Text © Transatlantic Press
All photographs ©Associated Newspapers Archive

A catalogue record for this book is available from the British Library.
ISBN 978-0-9557949-9-5

Printed in China

# Contents

Introduction                                      7

Part One   Fairy-tale Princess                    8

Part Two   Queen of Hearts                      134

Acknowledgments                                 224

# Introduction

On July 29, 1981 the "fairy tale" began when Lady Diana Spencer married Prince Charles in a spectacular ceremony at St. Paul's Cathedral, London. Diana was well-suited to her future role: her grandmother was a friend and lady-in-waiting to the Queen Mother; her father had been an equerry to King George VI and to the Queen; and Diana was born on the Queen's Sandringham estate.

Diana's relationship with Prince Charles began in the summer of 1980 while she was working at a private kindergarten. A romance swiftly blossomed despite the daily pressures from the media, intent on seeking out the Prince's future bride. Charles proposed in February 1981 and the marriage took place five months later. The couple honeymooned on the royal yacht *Britannia* and made their home at Highgrove, in Gloucestershire, with Kensington Palace as their London base.

In June 1982 their first son, William, was born, two weeks before Diana's twenty-first birthday, followed by Harry, in September 1984. Diana was determined to make the boys' lives as "normal" as possible and broke with royal tradition if necessary to achieve this.

On official engagements the Princess quickly demonstrated her compassionate nature, but felt she needed a more fulfilling role. In 1987 came the opportunity; HIV and AIDS sufferers were stigmatized and she saw the chance to break down the barriers created by ignorance and mistrust. Her work was a huge success and she eventually became involved with over one hundred charities.

However, the fairy-tale marriage was not to last. After several unhappy years Diana and Charles finally separated in 1992 and divorced in August 1996. The following summer Diana met Dodi Fayed. A whirlwind romance began and instantly attracted the attention of the press. On Saturday August 30, 1997 the paparazzi were waiting outside the Ritz Hotel in Paris, where Diana and Dodi were having dinner. Trying to avoid photographers, their Mercedes sped away and crashed in the Alma tunnel. Dodi and the chauffeur were killed instantly and although Diana was pulled out alive, she died in the early hours of Sunday morning.

News of her death shocked the world. The tributes of mourners created a sea of flowers around Kensington Palace and people wept openly on the streets. On the day of her funeral one million people lined the route, while millions more around the world watched on television.

Diana left a deep impression on everyone, and her legacy lives on. Her "beloved boys" have inherited her compassion and continue her charity work today, determined to keep their mother's memory alive.

This richly illustrated book, with hundreds of photographs selected from the archives of the *Daily Mail*, supported by an informative text, tells the story of a woman who captured the hearts of a generation.

## Part One

# Fairy-tale Princess

## Early years

Opposite: Diana Frances Spencer, aged nine, youngest daughter of Viscount Althorp, the eighth Earl Spencer. She was born on July 1, 1961 and raised at Park House on the Queen's Sandringham Estate in Norfolk, thus growing up in very close proximity to the Royal Family. Her grandmother Lady Ruth Fermoy was a close friend of the Queen Mother and Diana's young playmates included Princes Andrew and Edward. On the death of her grandfather in 1975, the family moved to Althorp House in Northamptonshire, the family seat.

Above: Diana boarded at Riddlesworth Hall near Diss and then followed her sisters to West Heath public school in Kent but after two attempts failed to secure any passes in her "O" Level exams. She did, however, excel at sport and was particularly noted for her ease and rapport with the elderly and handicapped people she visited as part of a school voluntary program. On leaving West Heath she spent a short time at a finishing school in Switzerland but finally settled in London after Earl Spencer purchased an apartment for her as a coming of age gift.

## First meeting

Opposite: Diana caught by press photographers in 1980, outside the door of her apartment at 60, Colherne Court, in London. During her time at West Heath Diana had idolized Prince Charles, covering her walls with his posters. He was a close friend of her elder sister Sarah and they finally met when she was sixteen, after he was invited to a shooting party on the Althorp Estate. A few years were to pass before they came together again at another shooting party in the summer of 1980, this time at Petworth.

Right: Lord Mountbatten had died the previous year and Diana spent much time with Charles offering condolences and speaking candidly to him about his emotions. She made an instant impact on the Prince and invitations to the opera, dinner, and then Balmoral soon followed. In Scotland the couple spent hours walking and fishing together. This media circus followed Diana relentlessly for the rest of the year, even while Prince Charles was in India and Nepal on official engagements.

## Nanny Diana

Opposite: When Diana settled in London she initially worked on a casual basis for friends, earning a pound an hour cleaning, waitressing at parties, and nannying. She then accepted a part-time post at the Young England kindergarten in Pimlico, a private pre-school for wealthy families. Diana was an instant hit showing a natural ability and rapport with young children and alongside this post also worked as a nanny for American businesswoman Mary Robertson, looking after her son Patrick. Outside work she had a busy social life partying, attending charity balls and spending weekends in the country.

Left: The infamous photograph of Diana in a diaphanous skirt as she supervised children from the kindergarten playing in St. George's Square.

### A royal engagement

Left and opposite: On Prince Charles's return from India, Diana joined the Royal Family for New Year at Sandringham. By now, both Charles and Diana were feeling the strain from the media's attention and Prince Philip wrote to his son asking him to consider Diana's feelings and make a decision. Charles returned to Britain and on February 6, 1981 invited Diana to Windsor Castle for a candlelit dinner, and formally proposed to her. Although he suggested she consider his request during her forthcoming trip to Australia with her mother, Diana accepted immediately. On February 24, after public speculation had reached fever pitch, the engagement was formally announced and the couple happily posed for photographers in the grounds of Buckingham Palace as Diana showed off her sapphire engagement ring surrounded with diamonds.

### First public engagement

Above: Diana at Sandown Park, watching Charles ride Good Prospect in the Grand Military Gold Cup. As soon as the engagement was announced Diana effectively become part of the Royal Family. The night before the announcement she had stayed at Clarence House, home of the Queen Mother, but was soon moved to an apartment in Buckingham Palace.

Opposite: Diana's first public appearance was soon scheduled in early March, a musical recital at Goldsmith's Hall in aid of the Royal Opera House Development Appeal. Diana had hastily visited Elizabeth and David Emanuel's design studio to choose a beautiful black strapless, taffeta gown for the evening.

## Out and about with her Prince

Opposite: In mid-March Charles left for an official visit that included Australia and New Zealand and was not due to return until early May. During this time Diana lived at the Palace and began to work with the Royal officials to organize their forthcoming wedding. She asked the Emanuels to design her dress and with help from her mother selected the final design. On Charles's return, the couple visited the nearby town of Tetbury to open a new operating theater at the local hospital.

Above: Charles and Diana visit St. Paul's Cathedral on June 11. Charles had deliberately chosen this venue over Westminster Abbey, preferring the architecture and acoustics. Diana was also busy organizing the refurbishment of Highgrove, where she and Prince Charles were due to live after the wedding. The Duchy of Cornwall had purchased this country house in 1980, as a private residence for the Prince of Wales.

## Pre-wedding nerves

Above: Diana and Sarah Ferguson at Guards Polo Club. The young bride-to-be had quickly gained the confidence of Sarah Ferguson, whose father, Major Ronald Ferguson, managed Charles's polo team. At weekends Diana would regularly watch her fiancé play.

Opposite: The months before the wedding were obviously very stressful for the young bride-to-be. Charles was away and the arrangements for the wedding had to be tempered with long-standing traditions overseen by the Lord Chamberlain, Lord Maclean. Diana could no longer spend time with her old friends and was visibly losing weight in the lead up to the day.

## A fairy-tale bride

Opposite and right: On Wednesday July 29, 1981, after five months of intense preparation and organization, the wedding day arrived. A public holiday had been declared and crowds began to line the processional route from Monday evening. It proved to be a quintessential summer's day and from early morning London was bathed in glorious sunshine. By the time Prince Charles left Buckingham Palace with his supporter, Prince Andrew, over one million people lined the route. Diana traveled to the cathedral with her father, Earl Spencer, in the Glass Coach and as she stepped out, finally revealed the long awaited wedding gown. She waved to the expectant crowds and then with her father, began the three-and-a-half-minute walk down the aisle to the sound of the *Trumpet Voluntary*. The service was conducted by Dr. Robert Runcie, the Archbishop of Canterbury who began his address, "Here is the stuff of which fairy tales are made: the Prince and Princess on their wedding day." Sarah Armstrong-Jones was chief bridesmaid, accompanied by four other bridesmaids and two pageboys.

## Prince and Princess of Wales

As part of the wedding ceremony, Diana had requested the hymn "I Vow to Thee My Country": Not only were the words appropriate, but it was also a favorite hymn of Lord Mountbatten's. The service was relayed to the crowds outside who applauded the Prince and Princess as they made their vows. Nerves obviously crept into the occasion as the Prince agreed to share Diana's wordly goods but not his own and she muddled his names. Diana's wedding dress had been made from forty-five feet of ivory silk taffeta with ten thousand pearls and sequins sewn onto the bodice and a twenty-five-foot train. On her head was the Spencer tiara, a family heirloom, and she carried a bouquet that included veronica and myrtle from the gardens at Osborne House on the Isle of Wight.

### While the world looked on

Above and opposite: After the service the radiant newlyweds emerged from the west door of the cathedral and were greeted by an amazing cacophony of noise as the crowds outside roared with delight. Horns, whistles, and rattles could be heard everywhere as they descended the steps of the cathedral and climbed into the waiting landau. On Diana's finger was the new wedding ring made from a nugget of Welsh gold, mined in 1923. It had previously been used for the wedding rings belonging to the Queen Mother, the Queen, Princess Margaret, and Princess Anne. Thus began a jubilant procession with members of the Royal Family following behind as they slowly wound their way back to Buckingham Palace. As many as 11,000 police were on duty at any one time and an estimated 750 million people around the world watched the event on television.

### Sealed with a kiss

Once the procession was safely inside the grounds of Buckingham Palace, the crowds poured down the Mall to surround the Palace. All were waiting expectantly for the traditional appearance on the balcony and just after one o'clock Charles and Diana emerged to greet a jubilant crowd. The cheers and applause were deafening and the young couple were clearly enjoying themselves. After much prompting from the well-wishers Prince Charles kissed his new bride and then after a record twenty-minute appearance, the family slipped quietly inside to begin their wedding breakfast while the rest of the country began their own celebrations. Across Britain people celebrated with street parties, barbecues and other special events to mark the occasion.

### "Just married"

Opposite: Later in the afternoon crowds began to reassemble in the Mall. At about 4.30 p.m. the Palace gates opened and the carriage bearing the Prince and Princess emerged, with some members of the Royal Family still showering them with rose petals. A huge cluster of blue and silver helium balloons with the Prince of Wales's feather emblem was attached to the back and, as it left the Palace, the placard "Just Married" could be clearly seen, craftily attached to the carriage at the last moment by Prince Andrew and Prince Edward. They made the journey to Waterloo Station where they were to catch a train to Romsey, in order to travel to Broadlands, home of the late Lord Mountbatten, where they were to stay for the next three days. This was followed by a two-week cruise around the Mediterranean on the Royal Yacht *Britannia*.

Right: When they returned from their cruise, the happy couple joined the rest of the Royal Family for the traditional annual holiday at Balmoral.

### First baby due

Above: A meeting backstage with Elizabeth Taylor, after a performance of *Little Foxes* at the Victoria Palace Theatre. In October 1981, Charles and Diana had left Balmoral to begin married life together. Although their official London home was to be in Kensington Palace, the apartments were still being decorated, so as a temporary basis, they moved into Buckingham Palace. The official functions swiftly began when they set out on a three-day tour of Wales at the end of the month. Anne Beckwith-Smith was appointed as lady-in waiting to offer support and companionship to the nervous young bride.

Opposite: Diana arrived at the Royal Opera House to watch the ballet *Romeo and Juliet*. It was soon evident that Diana felt at ease dispensing with the usual handshakes to reach out to touch and embrace people. The crowds adored her unreserved nature as she continued to greet people despite the freezing temperatures and torrential rain. The press soon noticed how pale she was looking and on November 5 her pregnancy was announced with the baby due the following summer. She suffered from severe morning sickness from very early on and as a result had to cancel many engagements.

### Proud parents

Opposite: On June 21 Diana gave birth to a son. The couple had already decided that their first baby would be delivered in hospital rather than at one of the Royal residences, which had previously been a Royal Family tradition. William was born at 9.03 p.m. at St. Mary's Hospital, Paddington, weighing 7lb 1oz. Prince Charles had been with Diana during the long sixteen-hour labor and finally emerged from the hospital later that evening to greet the waiting crowds. The new parents proudly took the young prince home the following evening.

Above: Five weeks after William's birth, Diana resumed public engagements when she attended the Falklands Thanksgiving Service at St. Paul's Cathedral. The Queen, who had ordered a 41-gun salute at Hyde Park and the Tower of London on the occasion of William's birth, was reported to have said "Thank goodness he hasn't got ears like his father!" Meanwhile, the redecoration of Kensington Palace had finally been finished in May 1982, so at last the couple were able to live in their own London home.

### Prince William Arthur Philip Louis

Opposite: William's christening was planned for August 4 and took place in the Music Room at Buckingham Palace with the Archbishop of Canterbury, Dr. Robert Runcie, leading the service. The prince was baptized William Arthur Philip Louis; the godparents were Lord Romsey, Sir Laurens van der Post, King Constantine, the Duchess of Westminster, Princess Alexandra, and Lady Susan Hussey. Royal tradition dictated that he wore a robe of Honiton lace originally made for Queen Victoria's children and he was baptized with water from the River Jordan.

Above: At first Diana looked after William herself but when he was ten weeks old, she hired nanny Barbara Barnes to assist her. Royal duties resumed when Diana visited Leatherhead in Surrey to open an extension to the Royal School for the Blind.

## Public duties

Above: The Prince and Princess of Wales were among those who welcomed Queen Beatrix and Prince Claus of the Netherlands when they landed at Westminster Pier to begin a two-day State visit. After William's birth, the Princess suffered badly from post-natal depression and quickly lost a great deal of weight, with rumors of bulimia beginning to circulate in the press. Nevertheless she continued with her public role.

Opposite: A radiant smile as Diana attends a concert at the Whitbread Brewery in London. In September, after the sudden death of Princess Grace of Monaco, Diana appealed directly to the Queen to allow her to attend the funeral on her own and represent the Royal Family. She had met Princess Grace the previous year during her first public engagement. Diana had been very nervous and the Princess had taken the time to reassure her; Diana had never forgotten that occasion.

## Tour of Wales

Opposite: The couple returned to Wales in November 1982 for a two-day tour of their own principality, including visits to Wrexham and Aberdovey. Charles had always taken his role as Prince of Wales seriously, learning the language, spending time at Aberystwyth University prior to his investiture, and holding many different posts across the country, including that of Colonel-in-Chief of the Royal Regiment of Wales.

Above: A windy day spent visiting the wreck of the *Mary Rose* in Portsmouth. The Prince and Princess had deliberately made Wales the first place they visited after their marriage and Diana had been granted freedom of the city of Cardiff.

## Missing William

Opposite: The Nightingale Home for the Elderly received a visit from Diana in February 1983. At the beginning of 1983, Charles and Diana had been on their first skiing holiday together. Leaving William at home with nanny Barbara, they traveled to Lech in Austria. Once again, the media followed them and at times Diana found their constant presence a real strain. Diana also missed six-month-old William dreadfully and the holiday confirmed her determination not to be separated from him unless it was unavoidable.

Right: A rather windswept Diana pictured at the Charlie Chaplin playground for handicapped children in Kennington Park, London. She had confessed to donning thermal underwear for such occasions.

### Royal waltz in Sydney

Left: Charles waltzes Diana around the dance floor at a charity ball in Sydney. In March 1983, Charles and Diana had begun a six-week tour of Australia and New Zealand. They cut straight through the Royal tradition of leaving children at home and insisted that William accompany them. It worked well. Nanny Barbara cared for William at a sheep station at Woomargama in New South Wales while his parents embarked on a grueling schedule of appearances, regularly returning to see him. Once again Diana was an instant hit with the people who loved her warmth and spontaneity. In the city of Melbourne a record crowd of 400,000 people lined the streets, while in Brisbane the walkabout had to be abandoned for fear of Diana being swallowed up into the crowd.

Opposite: As guest of honor, Diana attended the Variety Club Sunshine Club luncheon at the Guildhall, London.

## Most popular woman in the world

Above: At the Red Dragon Ball at the Grosvenor House hotel, Diana was greeted by Anwen Rees who was dressed in traditional Welsh costume. She gave the Princess a toy red dragon. At the end of April Charles and Diana were able to spend a ten-day vacation in the Bahamas, borrowing a villa from their friends, the Romseys. The media were still able to track the couple from a distance and photos appeared in the press of Charles and Diana walking on the beach holding hands and playing in the sea.

Opposite: Defying the rain, Diana met the crowds outside the Asian center in Walthamstow, London. In May, she and Prince Charles had embarked upon a seventeen-day tour of Canada where once again, Diana enthralled the waiting crowds. Her popularity around the world continued to grow: in an American poll she was dubbed "the most popular woman in the world" and in France *Paris-Match* claimed her popularity in the country outstripped that of Brigitte Bardot.

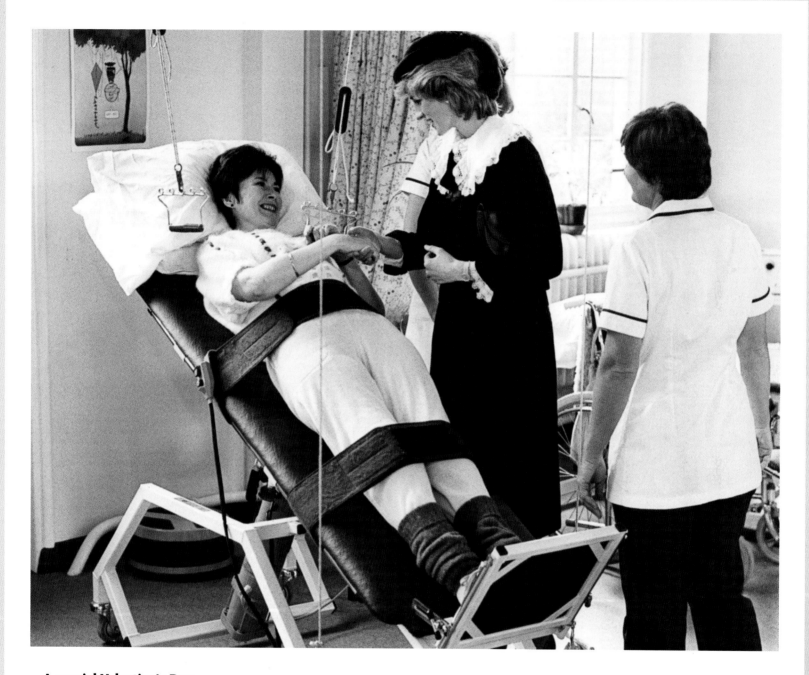

### A special Valentine's Day

At the beginning of 1984 Diana realized she was pregnant again. The announcement was deliberately made on Valentine's Day, with their second child due in September. Once more she suffered very badly with bouts of morning sickness that often lasted throughout the day but managed to maintain most of her engagements, although at times looking rather pale and queasy. A visit to the Royal National Orthopaedic Hospital in Stanmore to open a new £2 million spinal injuries unit gave her plenty of opportunity to laugh and joke with well-wishers and patients. Patient Pat Galimore (above), who had broken her back in a car accident discussed with the Princess the role husbands needed to play when a mother was unwell.

### President of the Royal Academy of Music

Above: In May 1984, Diana had the opportunity to met Luciano Pavarotti who was performing at a charity concert at the Royal Opera House, Covent Garden. He was to become one of her favorite performers. She was currently President of the Royal Academy of Music. As she continued with engagements, members of the public regularly gave her gifts for William and the new baby.

Opposite: A radiant mother-to-be, Diana watched her husband's polo team win 7–6 at Cirencester. During her second pregnancy, Diana chose to dress very differently. Unlike the first time, when she wore over-sized maternity clothes from the very beginning, this time she chose to wear clothes that concealed her shape, often asking Jaspar Conran to design them for her.

### Welcome Prince Harry

Above: On Saturday September 15, 1984, while at Windsor, Diana went into labor eleven days earlier than expected and was immediately driven to St. Mary's, Paddington, with a police escort. Members of the public and the media waited outside the hospital for news. Later that afternoon at 4.20 p.m., Prince Henry Charles Albert David was born, weighing 6lb 14oz. Early the following day, Prince Charles brought William to the hospital to meet his new younger brother, who was to be known as Prince Harry.

Opposite: Charles and Diana left the hospital later that afternoon to return to Kensington Palace.

## Dr. Barnardo's

Opposite: Once again, Diana resumed her public engagements soon after Harry's birth. In November the Princess went to the Dr. Barnardo's Centre in Newham, London, where she was able to meet children and staff to find out more about the charity's different activities first hand. She had recently become president of Dr. Barnardo's, taking over from Princess Margaret, a position she was to hold for twelve years, attending over one hundred events in total.

Above: Diana in Ealing in November 1984, visiting another Children's Centre. As usual, crowds of people turned out to wish her well and to congratulate her on the birth of a second son. She became very involved with Dr. Barnardo's, who were determined to shed their image as a Victorian orphanage and make the public aware that their aim was to help today's children with their many different problems.

## Sharing a joke

Above: A chance to share a joke with Dame Edna Everage (Barry Humphries) while illusionist Paul Daniels waits to be introduced. On December 21, Prince Harry's christening took place at St. George's Chapel, Windsor. His godparents were Prince Andrew, Bryan Organ, Gerald Ward, Lady Sarah Armstrong Jones, Carolyn Bartholomew, and Lady Celia Vestey.

Opposite: Crowds swamped the Princess as she arrived to launch the P & O liner *Princess Royal*. The following March one of her favorite designers, Bruce Oldfield, organized a gala fashion show as a fund-raiser for Dr. Barnardo's. Oldfield had been in foster care as a child and asked Diana to be guest of honor. Guests were charged £100 a ticket, and the event eventually raised over £200,000. Diana arrived at Grosvenor House wearing a stunning Oldfield gown and her presence immediately raised the profile of the charity.

## Rapturous cheers

Opposite: As part of her Dr. Barnardo's work, Diana spent a day at the charity's headquarters in Tanners Lane, Ilford. When she left, rapturous cheers were heard from the children living at the Barnardo's Village next door; they were there while waiting to be fostered or adopted. The Prince and Princess undertook a joint seventeen-day tour of Italy in April 1985, where once again the Princess's wardrobe was a major talking point. At every event she wore a dazzling designer outfit specifically created for the occasion. It was their first official tour together of a country outside the Commonwealth. Beginning in Sardinia the couple visited Florence, Sicily and then Rome where they attended a private audience with Pope John Paul II. When they reached Venice, the final leg of the tour, William and Harry flew out to join them so they could enjoy a brief family cruise around the Mediterranean aboard the Royal Yacht *Britannia*.

Right: A nautical theme was chosen for Diana's visit to the Isle of Wight in May.

## Chatting to the crowds

Opposite: During a visit to the Poolmead Centre of the Royal National Institute for the Deaf in Bath, Diana was quite happy to chat to one resident, Ian Forbes, through his open window. It was around this time that Diana played the role of matchmaker. Sarah Ferguson had been a long-standing friend of the Princess and they regularly met for lunch. In June Diana secured an invitation for Sarah to the Queen's Ascot Week house party at Windsor Castle. She also managed to seat her next to Prince Andrew at lunch; the couple were instantly attracted to each other and to Diana's delight, a whirlwind romance began.

Left: Diana opened the International Stoke Mandeville Games at the Ludwig Guttman Sports Centre, Stoke Mandeville. In July, she attended the sixteen-hour Live Aid concert held simultaneously in London and the JFK stadium in Philadelphia. Organized by rock star Bob Geldof, 1.5 billion people watched the concerts worldwide and a total of $40 million was raised. Diana gave her full support and backing to his plans and her enjoyment of the event was obvious as she bopped and clapped along to the music.

### Family cruise

Opposite:  August was traditionally time for the Royal Family's six-week holiday in Scotland. This year, after meeting at Southampton to board the Royal Yacht *Britannia*, the family cruised around the Western Isles before traveling to Balmoral where they would stay until October. By now William was three and Harry nearly one. Their parents continued to spend as much time with their children as they possibly could, dividing their time between Kensington Palace and their country home, Highgrove.

Left: A visit to the Remploy factory in Coventry.

## Miss Mynors' kindergarten

Opposite: It was now time for William to begin his education and again Charles and Diana rejected Royal tradition, sending him to school rather than having him educated at home. They were determined to keep his life as near normal as possible and provide opportunities for him to mix with his peers and make his own friends. They visited several schools and conducted a great deal of research, eventually choosing Miss Mynors' kindergarten in Notting Hill Gate, London.

Additional security systems were installed before he started in September 1985, joining the cygnets class with eleven other children.

Above: Diana chats to children in the crowd. She had a great empathy with young people, as well as with the elderly and the sick. She had described her own son, William, as "a very independent child—and very much an organizer."

## Clouds on the horizon

Above and opposite: A joke and a smile with patients at St. Joseph's Hospice in Hackney, East London. Diana had taken to the public side of royal life with ease but there were questions about her private life. In October Charles and Diana agreed to an exclusive interview with Sir Alastair Burnet. Rumors had been circulating that the marriage was in trouble and the Palace press office was determined to squash them. ITN agreed a fee of £1 million that would go straight to the Prince's Trust charity. During the program 20 million viewers tuned in to hear the couple vehemently deny any rumors of arguments and the many other claims that were circulating. In preparation for the interview Diana had been coached by Sir Richard Attenborough and was able to answer Burnet's questions clearly and rationally, also making it clear that she believed she received too much publicity in the press. The interview was subsequently linked to a fly-on-the-wall documentary that followed the couple for nearly a year, and a book written by Burnet.

### Dynasty Di

Opposite: An intimate moment between the Prince and Princess after a polo match at Werribee Park in Australia. Soon after the ITN interview Charles and Diana had set off for a tour of Australia and the United States of America. At a memorable White House ball, Diana danced with John Travolta and Clint Eastwood and met dancer Mikhail Barishnikov, telling him that in her teens she had waited outside Covent Garden stage door for his autograph. Eastwood cheerfully told the media afterwards, "She made my day." At the British Embassy in Washington Diana met up once again with her former employer Mary Robertson, and her son Patrick. Mary commented afterwards how much Diana had changed from the shy, quiet girl who had looked after her son five years ago into "this icon." *Time* magazine made the Royal tour their cover story and dubbed Diana "Dynasty Di."

Right: Diana chose a purple velvet-collared "teddy girl" suit to wear to a rock concert in Australia. Fashion writers dubbed the suit dowdy, showing how much she was constantly under scrutiny.

## A surprise appearance

Above: Diana greets her brother Charles, Viscount Althorp, at the Birthday Ball held at the Royal Albert Hall, in aid of the Birthright charity, and (opposite) a radiant Princess photographed at the Odeon, Leicester Square when she arrived for the premiere of *Santa Claus*. The Princess willingly lent her support to many charites, but Birthright was a cause that particulary struck a chord and with which she became much more involved.

Each December the Friends of Covent Garden traditionally held a VIP evening at the Royal Opera House with ballet dancers and singers reversing roles. Often a guest celebrity would make a surprise performance. For weeks, Diana had secretly rehearsed a dance routine with Wayne Sleep and just before the end of the show she slipped out of the Royal Box and appeared on stage in white satin. Much to the delight of the audience they performed a pas de deux to Billy Joels's "Uptown Girl" and afterwards received eight curtain calls and a standing ovation.

## A royal proposal

Opposite: Diana accompanied by Prince Andrew and Princess Anne. The romance between Prince Andrew and Diana's close friend Sarah Ferguson was blossoming. Sarah had been invited to spend the summer break with the Royal Family at Balmoral and the relationship was the subject of much media speculation. The couple spent a skiing holiday at Klosters with Charles and Diana and on March 19, Prince Andrew proposed to Sarah Ferguson at Floors Castle in Scotland. The wedding was planned for July 23 at Westminster Abbey.

Left: A visit to a playgroup in Islington, London.

## State visit

Right: Charles and Diana were at Victoria Station to meet the President of the Federal Republic of Germany and Freifrau von Weizsacker, who had arrived in Britain for a four-day State visit. Along with some other members of the Royal Family, they all traveled to Buckingham Place in a carriage procession.

Opposite: A smiling Princess at the Markfield project, North London.

### A grueling schedule

Above: Diana at the charity luncheon in aid of Save the Baby. In May Charles and Diana traveled to Vancouver, Canada, for the opening of Expo '86, then undertook a six-day tour of Japan. The country was at fever pitch; more people had watched the Royal wedding in Japan than in England. They underwent a punishing schedule covering 29 engagements and working in excess of twelve hours a day. Once again, Diana dressed carefully for each occasion and on arrival wore an outfit printed with the symbol of the rising sun. She watched a traditional tea party in Kyoto and was presented with a kimono.

Opposite: Just before Prince Andrew's wedding to Sarah Ferguson, Charles hosted a dinner for friends and family at the Rue St. Jacques restaurant in Charlotte Street in London. During the week the media had related tales of a visit by Sarah, Diana and comedienne Pamela Stephenson to Annabel's nightclub in Berkeley Square. Dressing up as policewomen and disguising themselves with wigs they made a light-hearted attempt to gatecrash Andrew's stag night.

### Enjoying the ballet

Opposite: As patron of the British Deaf Association, Diana attended the performance of *Ivan the Terrible* by the Bolshoi Ballet at the Royal Opera House in London. There was yet another chance to enjoy the ballet at the *London Standard* Ballet Awards at the London Coliseum (above). In November 1986 Charles and Diana toured the Arabian Gulf together. The visit was deemed a great success with the couple making perfect ambassadors despite the growing differences between them. During the tour they hosted a reception aboard *Britannia* for Saudi business leaders and the Sultan of Oman presented Charles with an Aston Martin and Diana with jewelry.

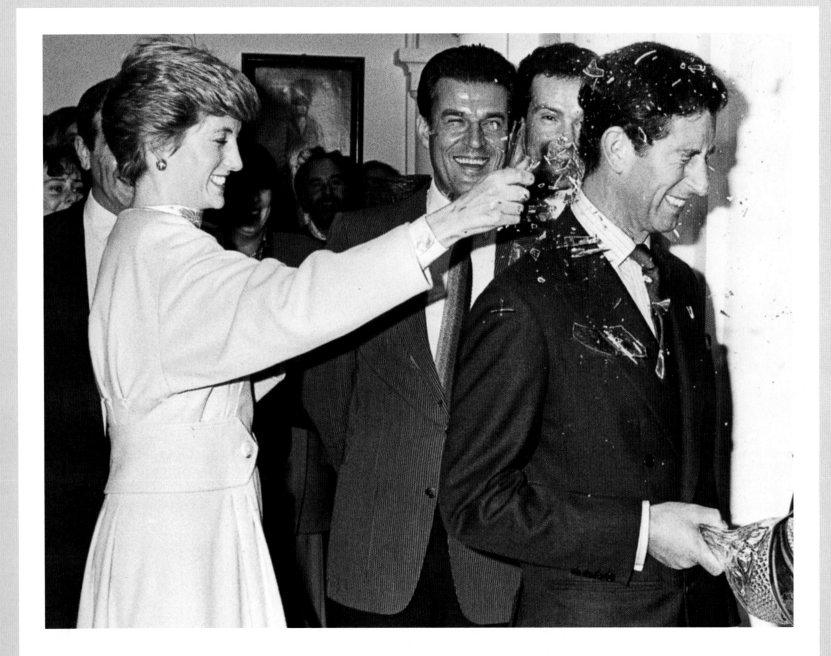

### Acting a part

Above: During a tour of Pinewood Studios to watch the new James Bond movie *The Living Daylights*, Diana took the opportunity to break a props bottle over her husband's head. Their son, William, was also appearing in a production; he was now coming to the end of his kindergarten education and in December he played the part of the innkeeper in the Christmas play. By now he had moved up to the "Big Swans" class and earned himself the nickname of "Basher"!

Opposite: Once again supporting the charity Birthright, Diana was at the Empire, Leicester Square, London, to attend a screening of the movie *The Mission*.

## An informal visit

Right: Diana makes a brief informal visit to the "Help the Aged" headquarters in Clerkenwell. The Princess would often make unofficial visits to the charities she supported, away from formality and the unrelenting eye of the media. In January 1987 her son William had begun his pre-prep education. Charles and Diana had selected Wetherby School in Notting Hill, London, which was run by Headmistress Miss Fredrika Blair Turner. She was a strong disciplinarian and had been given permission by Diana to smack William as a punishment if the need arose. Starting a new school coincided with the departure of his first nanny, Barbara Barnes. She was replaced by Ruth Wallace who the boys came to know as "Nanny Roof."

Opposite: A visit to open the new gallery at the National Maritime Museum in Greenwich, called "Discovery and Sea Power 1450–1700."

## Aids awareness

Above: Wearing a suit designed by Catherine Walker, Diana was at Sovereign Parade, Sandhurst, to plant a tree. In April she attended a luncheon (opposite) at Marlborough House to mark World Health Day. By 1987 Aids was known about but understood by few. It was referred to as the "gay plague"; most people were reluctant to come into contact with those with the virus and great stigma was attached to the disease.

Professor Mike Adler sent a request to the Palace for a member of the Royal Family to attend the opening of the first Aids ward at the Middlesex Hospital in London. Diana volunteered and on a highly successful visit she shook hands with patient Ivan Cohen; a photograph was immediately sent worldwide and helped to break down some of the myths about how the virus was spread.

## Happy Birthday!

Opposite: On her 26th birthday Diana spent the afternoon at Wimbledon watching the center court match between Ivan Lendl and Henri Leconte. She was with close friend Mrs. Catherine Soames, a regular tennis partner. The Princess was an avid tennis fan and attended matches at the tournament regularly. On this occasion she received a chorus of "Happy Birthday to You" from the crowd.

Above: Diana had known Mohamed Al Fayad since childhood, as he was a close friend of her father, Earl Spencer. On this occasion they were watching Charles's Windsor Park polo team beat the Guards and Charles scored four goals. The teams were playing for the Harrods Trophy but £30,000 was also raised for the Malcolm Sargent Cancer Fund for Children. Afterwards Al Fayad had organized a very emotional tea party for 50 children suffering from cancer, many of whom had very little time to live. Diana spent a long time talking to the children.

## Separate lives

Left: Charles and Diana had been to Pinewood Studios to watch *The Living Daylights* being made and in June they attended the premiere at the Odeon Leicester Square, afterwards meeting the new James Bond, Timothy Dalton. However, by mid-1987 the Prince and Princess were growing further apart. The majority of official functions were attended separately and Charles was living mainly at Highgrove, seeing their children at weekends. When they were together the tension and lack of affection between them was becoming more and more noticeable.

Opposite: At the Prince's Trust Concert held at the Wembley Arena Diana greeted ex-Beatles George Harrison and Ringo Starr. Eric Clapton and Midge Ure were also backstage waiting to be introduced.

### Freeman of the City

Right: On 22 July, Diana was made a Freeman of the City of London. Afterwards she made an acceptance speech to the 400 guests in the audience that included Prince Charles, Lord and Lady Spencer, Viscount Charles Spencer, Ruth, Lady Fermoy and Mrs. Frances Shand Kydd. She swore an oath of allegiance to the Queen and then spoke for a further three minutes, managing to conquer the initial nerves that made her hands shake. Afterwards she made another speech at a lunch held at the Mansion House.

Opposite: An off-the-shoulder gown for a function in aid of the London City Ballet and the Purcell School held at Charleston Manor, Sussex.

### Tragedy at Klosters

Opposite: A day at the Ascot races. 1988 began with Charles and Diana traveling to Australia to take part in the bicentennial celebrations in Sydney. However, in March tragedy struck. During a skiing holiday to Klosters a former Equerry to the Queen and a great friend of Charles, Major Hugh Lindsay, was killed in an avalanche after Prince Charles's party had gone off-piste. Patti Palmer-Tompkinson was seriously injured and Charles narrowly avoided injury. Lindsay had recently married and his wife Sarah was six months pregnant. Diana and Sarah Ferguson (above) were among those who flew back to RAF Northolt with the coffin carried from the plane by a guard of honor. Sarah Ferguson had also had a minor skiing accident but luckily had avoided any significant injury—she was four months pregnant at the time.

## Time for a break

Left: After the traditional Easter Service at St. George's Chapel, Windsor, Diana left the church with Prince William and Zara Phillips. Later that year, in August, Charles and Diana were guests of King Juan Carlos and Queen Sophia of Spain at the Marivent Palace in Majorca. Along with the boys they were able to enjoy a family vacation but rumors continued to circulate about the happiness of the Royal marriage. After the summer vacation Diana returned to England with the boys while Charles traveled to Italy and they were to spend their sixth wedding anniversary apart. The whole family went to Balmoral as usual but returned to London in mid-September as Harry was starting at Miss Mynors' kindergarten. Charles returned to Scotland, spending most of September and October there, while Diana remained in London with the boys.

Opposite: A strapless gown for the premiere of *Crocodile Dundee*.

### A new cousin

Opposite: On August 11, Sarah, Duchess of York, gave birth to her first daughter, Beatrice Elizabeth Mary, at the Portland Hospital in London. Diana was one of the first visitors, taking Princes William and Harry to meet their new cousin.

Left: It was a black tie occasion and so a tailored dinner suit with an emerald green waistcoat was the Princess's choice for a fund-raising grayhound meeting at Wembley.

### Committed to her role

Opposite: The Princess in a nautical mood, and (above) a visit to St. Catherine's Hospice in Crawley, Surrey. Diana was a very active supporter of Dr. Barnardo's, which had changed its names to Barnardo's in 1988. As part of her work as President, Diana was filmed in October visiting three fostered children in Tottenham, North London. The aim of the five-minute documentary was to show how under-privileged children could be helped if they were nurtured in the right environment. Bangie and Beryl Pringle had been fostering children for five years and were looking after three boys aged fourteen, nineteen and twenty who despite originally deemed "unfosterable" were now thriving. After filming had finished Diana stayed on to talk to the family asking about their lifestyles while they questioned her about hers. During the conversation she admitted that she did not do well at school, had failed her first driving test, and was hopeless at cooking. Producer Terry O'Reilly later commented on how committed she was to her role and the work of the charity, wanting to find out about its work as much as possible.

## Taking the helm

Opposite: At Cowes on the Isle of Wight, Diana named the new customs boat *The Vigilant*. It was the first of a new generation of cutters to travel at high speeds using advanced radar and communications to intercept drug smugglers. She had a ride on the craft and a turn at the helm, and despite gale-force winds asked the skipper to go full speed ahead. Diana was thrown backward and forward but managed to keep her footing. Later she admitted she had enjoyed the experience despite freezing cold temperatures.

Left: The Princess attended a meeting of the Child Accident Prevention Trust with actress Jane Asher, one of the trustees. She urged parents to make careful choices for their children's Christmas presents, avoiding dangerous toys. In November Charles and Diana had made an official visit to Paris where Diana asked to meet Professor Luc Montaigner, one of the scientists from the Institut Pasteur who was researching into Aids. On their return Charles celebrated his 40th birthday at Buckingham Palace, along with 600 guests. It was a glittering black-tie party but friends noticed how distant the couple were. Later that month Anthony Holden's biography of Prince Charles was serialized in the *Sunday Times*, timed to coincide with the birthday. Readers were stunned to hear that "their marriage has reached a stage of cold and mutual indifference."

### Flying solo

Opposite: In a black suit and hat trimmed with turquoise Diana attended the 1988 Christmas Day service at Sandringham. The following February she conducted her first solo tour abroad, visiting the United States of America. As well as attending gala dinners she was determined to the visit the sick and disadvantaged. The Henry Street shelter in Lower East Side Manhattan, a refuge for homeless and battered women, had attracted her attention; although one of the best social welfare programs in the States, they desperately needed to attract funding and needed a high-profile person to flag up their cause. During her visit to the shelter she characteristically spent most of the time talking to the families and asked countless questions. She then visited the Harlem Hospital Center in New York, where she happily cuddled a seven-year-old boy who was HIV-positive. Many Americans were unaware of these children's needs and soon offers of foster families flooded in. Later that month the Princess spent time at Mildmay Mission Hospital in Bethnal Green, London, meeting patients suffering from Aids. Medical director Dr. Veronica Moss was full of praise as Diana laughed and joked with patients and held their hands.

Right: Topped with a baseball cap, Diana drops Harry off at Miss Mynors' kindergarten to begin his last term at the school.

## Family time

Opposite: An eager Prince Harry rushes into the Palace Theatre to watch his brother, William, appear in the school concert. In March Charles and Diana undertook an official tour of the United Arab Emirates. Diana had obviously been versed on Arab protocol and during a desert picnic sat demurely on floor cushions carefully using her right hand to eat, as Arab custom dictates. In Dubai she was entertained with camel racing and afterward she asked why the riders never fell off. Much to her amusement she was then proudly shown how the seven-year-old riders' bottoms were securely attached to the saddles with Velcro! After the tour ended the couple left separately; Charles traveled on to Saudi Arabia while Diana returned to England.

Right: A wave to the crowds from four-and-a-half-year-old Harry when he attended the Easter Service at St. George's Chapel, Windsor. Earlier in the month Diana had made an impromptu visit to Mayday Hospital in Thornton Heath to meet survivors of the Purley train crash; six people had died in the accident and over 80 were injured.

**Turning Point**

Above: Diana was Patron of Turning Point, a charity that aimed to help people with alcohol and drug problems and those with mental health issues and learning disabilities. In June she went to Hackney to open Lorne House Centre, a center created by a collaboration between Turning Point, the Guinness Trust, and the Mental Health Foundation.

Opposite: The Princess in Hyde Park taking the salute for the march past of the Combined Cavalry: the "Old Comrades" parade.

## Wetherby School

Opposite: The Wetherby School Sports day was held in June and Diana was always a keen and successful contender in the mothers' race. The previous year she had won the 80-yard sprint, earning her the nickname of "Fly-Di." This year she came a very credible second in a field of about 40 mothers.

Right: Harry was now coming up to five and he was due to join his brother William at Wetherby School. He began four days before his birthday, albeit a couple of days late, owing to a viral infection. Once again, Headmistress Fredrika Blair-Turner came out to meet the family. Harry was due to attend for mornings only until the half-term break.

## Diana's brother marries

Opposite: On September 16, 1989 Diana's brother Charles married Catherine Victoria Lockwood (known as Victoria), the daughter of a civil aviation executive, at the Church of St. Mary at Great Brington in Northamptonshire on the Althorp Estate. Prince Harry had turned five the day before and was chosen to be pageboy at the wedding so William arrived separately with his parents.

Above: Diana and her mother Mrs Frances Shand Kydd enter the church. Diana's mother had divorced Earl Spencer when Diana was eight and subsequently married Peter Shand Kydd, the heir to a thriving wallpaper business. Earl Spencer had won custody of the children but they saw their mother regularly. Frances and Peter Shand Kydd had, however, divorced the previous year.

## Motorfair treat

Opposite: Diana and William sped into the Motorfair at Earls Court for a private unscheduled visit. The first car he wanted to see was the Ferrari Testarossa at £107,000 and capable of speeds of 180 m.p.h. However, he eventually came down to earth and bought a Corgi model of a BBC "Roadshow" Seddon-Atkinson transporter.

Right: The Princess photographed in a dramatic red suit at RAF Wittering. Diana had just been appointed as president of the Royal Academy of Dramatic Arts and in November took on her initial task to install actor John Gielgud as the academy's first honorary fellow in recognition of his life's work. During the ceremony Gielgud spoke of their new roles as "venerability and wisdom on one hand and youth and exquisite beauty on the other," causing the delighted Princess to blush.

## Lady in red

Left: The Princess chose a stunning red gown to attend the premiere of *When Harry Met Sally* at the Odeon in Leicester Square. Afterward she met the leading stars, Billy Crystal and Meg Ryan. The film had already grossed $60 million in the States but crucially the premiere successfully raised £50,000 for the charity Turning Point. She and Charles had toured Indonesia and Hong Kong together in November. In Jakarta the Princess again flouted protocol and visited the Sitanala leprosy hospital, happily chatting to patients and touching them without any fear or prejudice. At the hospital she spotted a bowling lawn and immediately set up an impromptu match, proving to be a very accurate shot. In Hong Kong, after a traditional welcome ceremony performed by hundreds of children and dragon dancers, she continued with several charity engagements that included the Hong Kong Red Cross, the Helping Hand senior citizens center and a visit to the Shek Kwu Chau community for recovering drug addicts.

Opposite: On Remembrance Sunday the Princess laid a wreath at the Guards' Chapel in Wellington Barracks, London.

### Supporting role

Opposite: Continuing to support patients with HIV and Aids, the Princess opened the Rodney Porter Ward at St. Mary's Hospital in Paddington, a joint venture between the NHS and Aids charities to specialize in treatment of the virus. She initially toured the hospital to gain further insight into the research programs and then took the opportunity to meet some of the patients, spending a great deal of time talking to them.

Above: The Princess wore a striking outfit for the traditional walk to church on the Sandringham Estate on Christmas Day.

### Patron of the British Deaf Association

Above: A visit to a day center for young homeless people in Adelaide Street, London. Diana's strong interest in charities had continued to grow and she now saw working as patron and fund-raiser to be her major role. She had been Patron of the British Deaf Association for seven years and January 1990 marked the beginning of the centenary year for the charity.

Opposite: Diana was introduced to (left to right) Sally Field, Olympia Dukakis, Daryl Hannah and Julia Roberts after the premiere of *Steel Magnolias*.

## Caribbean holiday

Opposite: Diana strides along a beach in the Virgin Islands. On March 23, 1990, Prince Andrew's wife Sarah had given birth to their second daughter, Eugenie Victoria Helena, at the Portland Hospital, London. After seeing their new niece the Prince and Princess, accompanied by William and Harry, had flown out to the Caribbean for a spring vacation.

Left: Diana took the opportunity to re-visit Lorne House, the hostel run by Turning Point for those with drug- and drink-related problems that she had opened in June 1989. That day the temperatures soared into the eighties and after the visit she abandoned her original schedule and spent extra time talking to the crowds who had gathered in the courtyard waiting to see her, despite the sweltering heat.

## Royal visit to Hungary

Opposite: Continuing to support one of her favorite charities Diana attended a day conference on "Women, Aids and the Future," at London's Commonwealth Institute, organized by the National Aids Trust. That summer the Prince and Princess made a visit to Hungary, a country that had recently been freed from Communist control. On arrival at the airport, Diana quietly consoled the wife of President Goncz who had been moved to tears by the occasion. During the tour Diana visited the Peto Institute, a world center for the treatment of children with cerebral palsy and other physical disabilities. There she learnt about the conductive education that it delivered, providing a therapeutic regime to give physically disabled children greater mobility. As a result of this visit she was soon to take on the role of Patron of the Birmingham Foundation for Conductive Education.

Right: San Lorenzo's restaurant in Beauchamp Place, London, was always one of Diana's favorites. The Italian owner Mara Berni fiercely protected Diana's privacy and it was one public place in which she could relax. On this occasion it was the venue for lunch with her brother Charles. His wife Victoria was expecting their first baby at the end of the year.

### Standing ovation

Right: Eight hundred delegates gave Diana a standing ovation at the centenary congress for the British Deaf Association. As part of her role as patron she had been learning British Sign Language and had delivered her speech in sign language, giving an immaculate performance.

Opposite: On June 28 Prince Charles broke his arm in two places after falling from a horse during a game of polo. Doctors at Cirencester hospital decided to reset it without pinning, but after spending the summer in continual pain he eventually saw a doctor recommended by his friencd Patti Palmer-Tompkinson. The arm had not healed properly and needed further surgery at the Queen's Medical Centre, Nottingham, in early September. During visits to the hospital to see her husband, Diana met the family of Dean Woodward, who had been seriously injured in a car crash the previous month and was in a coma in intensive care. Diana regularly visited and phoned him when he eventually emerged from his coma in October.

## A busy September

Opposite: Diana arriving at the Queen's Medical Centre, bringing William and Harry to visit their father. After the treatment the Prince was still very weak and was taken by helicopter back to Highgrove to convalesce. In the same month William began his prep school education at Ludgrove School in Berkshire. The school where he was to become a boarder was chosen for several reasons: it was reasonably close to Kensington Palace and Highgrove, had an excellent reputation for sport and a friendly atmosphere, and was reasonably secluded and set in grounds of 130 acres, which would afford William the privacy he needed.

Right: September was a busy month for the boys. It was Harry's sixth birthday and his treat was a surprise visit to the Battle of Britain 50th anniversary exhibition with a group of school friends. They were shown how to operate a World War II Bofors anti-aircraft gun and had the chance to sit in a Harrier jump jet. From an early age Harry had shown a keen interest in the military, collecting toy soldiers and memorabilia. His aim as a child was to join the parachute regiment when he grew up.

## Grandma's House

Opposite: Continuing to support the charity Birthright, Diana here visits a supermarket in Southport to launch their new booklet on healthy eating for pregnant women. In October, she made a solo trip to Washington, D.C. to attend a fund-raising gala as Patron for the London City Ballet. Although in the States for under twenty-four hours Diana also visited Grandma's House, a home in a deprived area for children with Aids. A three-year-old girl who was dying wished for a ride in Diana's car, which was immediately granted, but Diana was left close to tears afterwards.

Above: Harry joined his mother and William to carry out his first official function. The memorial service held at St. Paul's Cathedral was for the 1,002 firefighters who died in the London Blitz. He was rewarded afterwards with the chance to climb aboard a restored Leyland Metz fire engine that had been in service during World War II.

## Unhappy Marriages

Left: On a visit to Colchester Diana was greeted by Lady Amanda Ellingworth, of the Guinness Trust. Meanwhile, it was gradually beginning to emerge that the marriage between Prince Andrew and Sarah, Duchess of York, was starting to flounder. Owing to his Royal Navy commitments Andrew spent very little time at home with his wife and Sarah rapidly became frustrated about this. She and Diana engaged in long, frequent phone calls as they discussed their respective husbands and their unhappiness in their marriages.

Opposite: Supporting two charities, the Prince's Trust and Birthright, the Princess attends a concert by the London Symphony Orchestra at the Barbican.

# Part Two

# Queen of Hearts

## Royal Christening

Opposite: A visit to the Royal Lancaster Hotel. Later that same month the family attended the christening of Princess Eugenie, the daughter of Prince Andrew and the Duchess of York. She was baptized at the St. Mary Magdalene Church in Sandringham on December 23, the first member of the Royal Family to have a public christening.

Right: Diana attended the premiere of *Hobson's Choice* wearing a stunning green gown.

## Gulf War

Left: The Gulf War had broken out in August of the previous year and the air campaign, codenamed Operation Desert Storm, began in January 1991. In total over 40,000 troops were mobilized during the war. In January Diana inspected the graduates at Sandhurst military academy and sent good luck messages to Britain's armed forces, only too aware that many of the young cadets would be going straight to the Gulf.

Opposite: A visit to the FACTS Health co-ordination center in London.

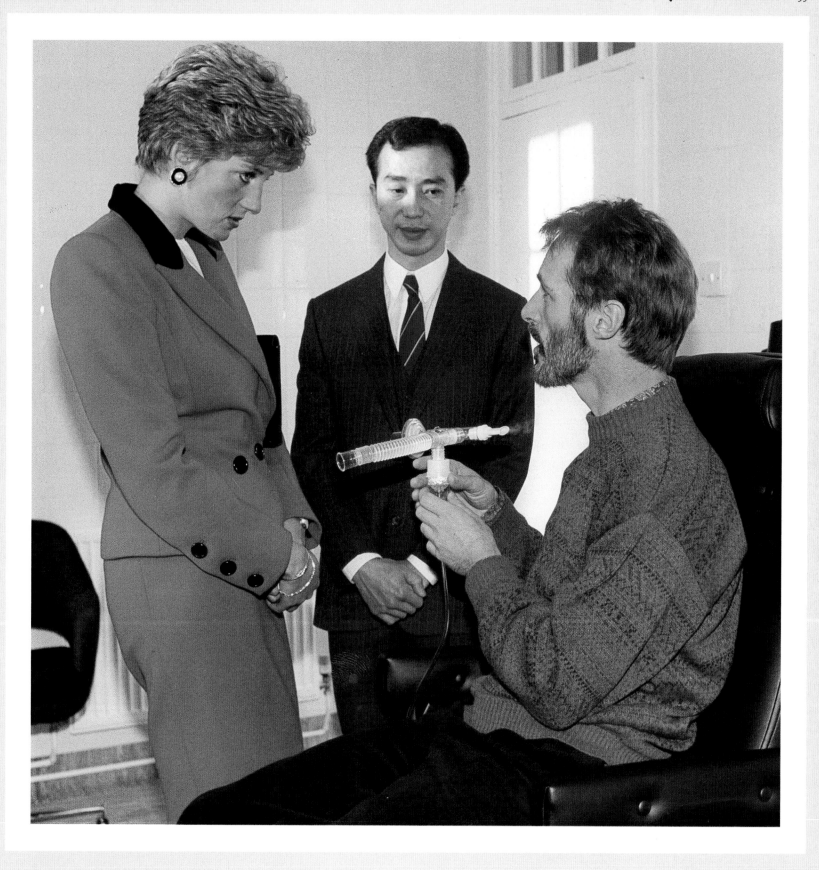

## Alton Towers

Above: Diana often took the boys to Alton Towers—one of their regular treats that she enjoyed planning. While there she insisted that they be treated like any other children and so stood in line for rides with everyone else and had no special privileges.

Opposite: Twelve-year-old Claire Cowdrey presented the Princess with a bouquet of flowers at the Children of Eden gala performance at the Prince Edward Theatre.

### Helping the Aged

Left: *LA Story* received its Royal premiere at the Canon in Shaftesbury Avenue, and Diana wore a beautiful cream chiffon beaded gown, designed by Catherine Walker. The movie featured Steve Martin, who also wrote the script and produced the picture, appeaing alongside his wife at the time, Victoria Tennant.

Opposite: At the Mansion House in London, Diana attended a dinner to mark the launch of ReAction Trust, a venture between industry and the Help the Aged. In her speech she asked people to consider the contribution that older people could make to society.

### Keeping fit

Above: Diana was always a keen swimmer, but toward the end of the eighties she also began to regularly visit gyms to keep fit and tone her body. Her sister-in-law Sarah, who she had encouraged to exercise after the birth of her second child, often accompanied her. Diana eventually decided to engage fitness instructor Carolan Brown who would visit the Princess at Kensington Palace so she could follow an exercise regime with greater privacy.

Opposite: Casual dress for the Royal mum who had just dropped six-year-old Harry at Wetherby School, after the Easter break.

## Professional ambassadors

Left: Although their marriage was rapidly disintegrating, the Prince and Princess were excellent ambassadors and always strived to be professional when embarking on Royal duties. During their visit to Brazil in April, they were able to appear in front of the media giving the impression that all was well.

Opposite: In May, Diana attended The Simple Truth charity concert at Wembley Arena. The event, which included performances from Sting and Rod Stewart, raised funds for the International Committee of the Red Cross. Screened to over 300 million television viewers across 37 countries worldwide, it urged viewers to pledge money to the charity to raise funds to assist Kurdish refugees in northern Iraq. The concert was organized by Jeffrey Archer.

## Knockout prince

Above: The annual Mothers' race at Wetherby school. On June 3, 1991, Prince William was accidentally hit on the head with a golf club by a school friend. William was knocked unconscious and the wound bled profusely. He was rushed to the Royal Berkshire Hospital but after a CT scan doctors recommended an immediate transfer to The Great Ormond Street Hospital for Sick Children. The accident had caused a depressed fracture of the skull and he needed a seventy-minute operation to repair the damage, but made a full recovery.

Opposite: After a charity performance of *Tango Argentino*, a spectacular dance show at the Aldwych Theatre, Diana was introduced to Elton John. The proceeds from the event went to the National Aids Trust.

## Thirtieth birthday

In July 1991 Diana turned thirty and the press was full of conflicting reports about the plans for her birthday. Some reported that Charles did not want to attend any celebrations while others claimed that Diana refused to accept his offer of a lavish party. Diana finally spent the day attending a lunch held at the Savoy Hotel for the children's hospice, Rainbow House. Twelve-year-old Sharon Carter, who suffered from cystic fibrosis, helped Diana blow out thirty candles on her birthday cake. The following week the Prince and Princess attended the Gala performance of Verdi's *Requiem* (opposite). The performance was sponsored by *The Sunday Times* and was planned to commemorate the Princess's birthday.

Left: The Prince and Princess attended a function at the Mansion House. The Queen was also present and Royal protocol demanded that Diana curtsey to her mother-in-law.

### Diana's mercy mission

Opposite: After the summer break at Balmoral Diana and the boys flew back with Prince Andrew and his daughters. During the holiday Diana had made a mercy mission back to London, driving 550 miles through the night. Her friend Adrian Ward-Jackson, an art dealer and governor of the Royal Ballet, had contracted HIV and in the spring of 1991 his condition began to deteriorate. Diana had been a frequent visitor to his apartment, but on August 19 she received a phone call to say the last rites had just been administered. Unable to find a plane, she drove to London herself to be beside him. He eventually died four days later. In her haste Diana had left without requesting permission from the Queen as was the custom. It was not only Diana's friends who benefited from her caring nature—she offered a moment of comfort for many sick people, including this severely disabled patient (above) at the Royal Hospital and Home, Putney.

## Tears and laughter

Opposite: Harry's seventh birthday treat took place within the grounds of Kensington Palace. To the delight of Harry and his friends a team of police dog-handlers put on a slapstick display, pretending to be cops and robbers. The dogs broke up fights between the policemen who were wielding baseball bats. Aunt Sarah and Harry's two cousins, Beatrice and Eugenie, were there to enjoy the celebrations.

Above: The Princess aboard a helicopter over Niagara Falls during the tour of Canada in October 1991. Earlier in the month news had reached Diana's family that five-year-old Leonora Knatchbull, great-granddaughter of Lord Mountbatten, had died after fighting cancer for the last fourteen months. Her parents Lord and Lady Romsey were great friends of Charles and Diana and the Princess had visited Leonora in hospital just before her death.

### Grooming the future king

Left: The whole family took part in the Canada tour. It was to be the start of a program of grooming for William as he gradually began to understand his future role. For security reasons William and Harry had flown out a day earlier than their parents and then had to wait while the Prince and Princess took part in a lengthy reception before they could join them again.

Opposite: At Milestone House, Diana sat down for tea with a lady suffering from Aids. She was also due to attend a conference organized by the National Aids Trust. There she listened to teenagers' views on how to improve sex education to protect teenagers from potentially contracting the disease. She made copious notes and met them more informally afterwards.

### Sharing the challenge

World Aids Day has been held on December 1 every year since 1988, originating from the World Summit of Ministers of Health on Programs for Aids Prevention. In 1991 the theme was "Sharing the Challenge" and Diana attended the *Dance for Life* event at her Majesty's Theatre. The program featured the Royal Ballet and dancers from the theater shows *Cats* and *Phantom of the Opera*. A total of £150,000 was raised for Crusaid. On Diana's arrival at the theater (opposite), four-year-old Nicola Gerry presented the Princess with flowers and asked for a kiss in return. After the performance Diana met the show's dancers including Darcey Bussell, Principal Dancer with the Royal Ballet (above).

## Going separate ways

Right: In February 1992, Charles and Diana visited India together. During the tour it became clear that the marriage was not working well, with the Prince and Princess no longer able to hide their differences. The majority of their schedules were separate, with Charles representing British business while Diana toured hospitals and charitable institutions. During a solo visit to the Taj Mahal, a monument erected by Mogul Emperor Shah Jahan as a memorial to his wife, a series of pictures issued by the press showed a lonely-looking woman.

Opposite: The Prince and Princess were determined to keep life for the two young princes as "normal" as possible. Diana would give William and Harry the same opportunities that any other child would have, on day trips and treats. One Sunday afternoon she and the boys were seen lining up at MacDonald's in Kensington High Street in London, with the other customers seemingly unaware of their presence.

### The untouchables

Opposite: During the tour of India, Diana again deliberately drove through prejudice by meeting the "untouchables," a disabled group from the lowest Indian caste. As they reached out to touch her ankles she moved closer, holding their hands in greeting. The Princess was patron of Help the Aged, who ran the center while also helping a total of 6,000 elderly people throughout India.

Above: On February 13, two days after Diana's visit to the Taj Mahal, Charles was playing in a polo match and Diana was invited to present prizes to the winning team. During the match Charles scored a brilliant goal, taking his team to victory. As he moved to kiss his wife after the match she deliberately turned her head to avoid him. The media were waiting for a classic romantic picture to run for Valentine's Day, but released the photograph the next day with reports of their failing marriage.

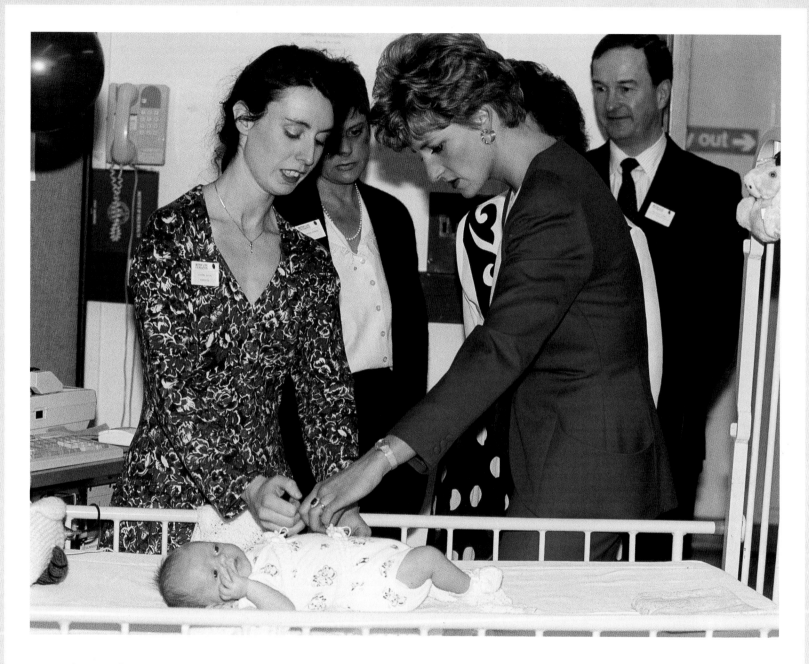

### Meeting Mother Teresa

Opposite: During the visit to India Diana had toured Mother Teresa's orphanage and hospice. The following month the Princess flew out to Rome to meet the diminutive nun and to hear more about her charitable work with the poor and sick of India.

Above: A chance to study the medical work at the Institute of Child Health. Meanwhile Diana's old friend Dr. James Colthurst had been

working with freelance writer Andrew Morton on her biography. The Princess spent many hours with Colthurst making tape recordings about her life, and friends such as Angela Serota and Carolyn Bartholemew gave their accounts to Morton. While the Princess was in India, Morton and his publisher, Michael O'Mara, began to approach newspapers to sell the serial rights to the book.

## Diana's father dies

Left: On March 28 Diana flew to Lech for a skiing holiday with Charles and the boys. However, it was tragically cut short when news broke that Diana's father, Earl Spencer, had died of a heart attack aged sixty-eight. Diana immediately flew home on one of the Queen's Flight accompanied by Prince Charles. The funeral was held at the Church of St. Mary at Great Brington on the Althorp Estate, where her brother had married three years earlier. Her father's ashes were buried in the family vault. Charles attended the funeral with Diana, although they traveled separately.

Opposite: In May a memorial was held for the late Earl Spencer at St. Margaret's, Westminster. Friends and family gathered to celebrate his life in a service led by the Rev. Dr. Donald Grey, Canon of Westminster. Robin Leigh-Pemberton, Governor of the Bank of England and an old school friend of the Earl, gave the address.

### Three marriages in trouble

Above: The traditional Easter service at Windsor. By now there were three Royal marriages in difficulty. During the previous year Prince Andrew and Sarah had continued to grow apart and in March 1992 their official separation had been announced. Princess Anne and Mark Phillips had announced their intention to separate three years earlier and in April 1992 the marriage was officially dissolved. To complete the trio, Charles and Diana's marriage was now hanging by its final thread.

Opposite: In May Diana completed a solo visit to Egypt. Charles traveled on the same plane of the Queen's Flight but disembarked at Ankara for a private vacation. During the brief tour she met President Hosni Mubarak and his wife and spent her time in the country combining diplomatic duties with sightseeing.

## Morton biography

Above: On June 7, 1992, *Diana: Her True Story*, by Andrew Morton, was serialized in *The Sunday Times*. Diana and Charles were both at Highgrove that morning but Diana hurried back to London. The book detailed Diana's bulimia, her feelings of abandonment, and Charles's affair with Camilla Parker Bowles. Publication put the marriage under further strain; later that month the Prince and Princess attended the Garter Ceremony at Windsor Castle but traveled separately and were barely speaking.

Opposite: Diana stops to admire the medals of one of the Chelsea pensioners on parade at the Royal Hospital Chelsea.

## Attempts at reconciliation

Despite the serialization of the book, Royal events continued as if nothing had happened. The following Saturday Diana was present on the Buckingham Palace balcony for the Trooping the Colour ceremony. The second installment was published the following day on June 14, when the Royal family were all at Ascot. The next day Charles and Diana met with the Queen and Prince Philip to discuss their marriage. Diana denied being involved with the book and the Queen suggested a family vacation to try to repair the marriage. Diana agreed to her requests and also continued her planned program of charity functions. She was asked to make a keynote speech for a Turning Point conference (left), but had become very distressed after watching a video presentation, needing time to compose herself first before she could speak.

Opposite: Diana accepted a bouquet of flowers from two-year-old Jade Symons during a visit to the Royal Albert Hall. Later that same month Mary Robertson, her former employer, was in England and arranged to have lunch with Diana at Kensington Palace.

## More revelations

Opposite: The Princess surrounded by children at a Barnardo's conference. Prince Harry had just completed his final term at Wetherby, and in September was due to join his brother, William, as a boarder at Ludgrove School.

Right: Perfectly co-ordinated as ever, the Princess was present for the opening night of the Australian ballet at the London Coliseum. That summer the whole family gathered at Balmoral for the traditional break, but further revelations in the press were to come. In August the *Mirror* published topless photographs of the Duchess of York having her toes sucked by Johnny Bryan, her financial adviser. Sarah immediately left Balmoral with her daughters. A few days later the *Sun* published the "Squidgygate" tapes in full. These were transcripts of an intimate conversation between Diana and James Gilbey, a used-car salesman and an old friend from her bachelor days, which had been recorded by a radio ham in January 1989. In them, Gilbey had continually referred to Diana as "Squidgy."

## Private princess

Opposite: The Princess smiled at waiting crowds as she entered the Royal Albert Hall for the First Night of the Proms. The press were still following the Royal marriages and author Penny Junor, who had previously written a biography about Prince Charles, published an article in the newspaper *Today* entitled "Charles: His True Story." She defended the Prince, mentioning his "sense of betrayal" over Diana's actions, and describing a private Diana unlike the lady the public saw. Meanwhile Camilla Parker Bowles was under constant pressure from the press.

Above: At the end of July a dinner was held to celebrate the fortieth anniversary of the Queen's accession to the throne. Charles and Diana attended together and the following month took the family vacation that the Queen had suggested. Flying to Greece they began a cruise in the Ionian Sea on a luxury cruise yacht called the *Alexander*. It had been lent to them by John Latsis, an oil tycoon and family friend. Despite their stunning surroundings, the vacation did nothing to heal the rift between the Royal couple.

## "Annus horribilis"

Left: A dazzling red gown for the royal charity performance of *Just Like A Woman*. The evening was a fund-raiser for leukemia research and Diana took the opportunity after the performance to meet the film's star, Julie Walters, and her daughter Maisie who suffered from the disease. In mid-November Diana made a solo visit to Paris. It was very successful and included a long meeting with President Mitterand and his wife Danielle at the Elysée Palace. *Paris-Match* featured her visit on the front page with the headline "Courage Princesse!" On her return she refused to join a weekend party at Sandringham and instead took the boys to Windsor. However, that weekend Windsor Castle caught fire and it was four days later, during a speech at the Guildhall, that the Queen referred to 1992 as her *"annus horribilis."*

Opposite: Charles and Diana arrived at Westminster Abbey together for the commemoration service of the 50th anniversary of the battle of El Alamein. Camilla Parker Bowles was also at the service with her father Major Bruce Shand, who had won the Military Cross. In mid-November the *Daily Mirror* had run an article entitled "Camilla Confidential" that included quotes from a conversation between Charles and Camilla from an undisclosed source.

## The pretence is over

Above: Diana enjoying a joke with Jackie Charlton at the Queen's 40th Anniversary Gala at Earls Court. By now the marriage was all but over. Diana had agreed to the Queen's request that she and Charles continue with the four-day tour of South Korea that was already planned. They were no longer able to hide their feelings and were christened "The Glums" by the press, their body language revealing all. Diana traveled back alone while Charles flew on to Hong Kong.

Opposite: During an AIDS conference, Diana was given high praise from the Junior Health Minister Baroness Cumberledge for the influence she had had on government policy.

### Moving on

Left: The Princess pictured deep in thought at the Welsh Guards Memorial Service. On November 25 Charles finally told Diana of his desire for a separation, to which she agreed. He immediately removed his possessions from Kensington Palace while she vacated Highgrove. Initial legal discussions then began over the care of the children, finances, and also Diana's future role within the Royal family.

Opposite: Continuing her work with Turning Point, Diana met some of the charity's sponsors at the International Convention Centre in Birmingham and viewed a display about Drugs Prevention Week.

## Separation announced

On December 9 Prime Minister John Major announced in the House of Commons the separation of the Prince and Princess of Wales. He insisted there would be no divorce and in the event of Charles becoming King, she would become Queen—drawing a gasp from listening MPs. The previous day Diana had traveled down to Ludgrove to explain their decision to William and Harry. William response was to tell his mother "I hope you will both be happier now." The same month Princess Anne's divorce from Mark Phillips was finalized and she married Commander Tim Laurence.

Above: Diana with the boys and their personal detective at Thorpe Park in January 1993. After their official separation Charles had taken the boys to Sandringham for Christmas while Diana spent the holiday at Althorp with her brother's family. Since her father's death Charles had inherited his title and the family estate, becoming the ninth Earl Spencer.

## Facing stormy waters

Opposite and above: Diana and the boys took full advantage of the Hudson Rafters Race water rides, again adhering to her policy that they stood in line along with all the other children receiving no special treatment. A major part of the separation agreement had been over Charles and Diana's access to the boys to minimize the effect the split would have on them. Another aspect had been the division of their staff. Jane Strathclyde had traveled from St. James's Palace to instruct the Highgrove employees; they were allocated jobs without any choice—such as butler Paul Burrell, who was asked to uproot his family to move to a post at Kensington Palace with the Princess.

### A royal soaking

Diana at Thorpe Park (opposite), soaked but happy, and on walkabout in Cambridge town center (above). In March 1993, the Princess went to Nepal with Lynda Chalker, Minister for Overseas Development, to view the British aid projects as had been previously planned. However, earlier in the year, on January 13, yet another bombshell had been dropped— the full transcript of secretly recorded tapes of conversations between Charles and Camilla was published in the *Sunday People* and the *Sunday Mirror*. Charles was abroad at the time but Camilla was immediately besieged by photographers. The tapes had been recorded in January 1989 by a radio ham, who kept them secret until the "Squidgy" tapes were released, but then realized the cash potential of his recordings. They had been the source of the quotes in the *Mirror* the previous November and revealed an intimate conversation between two people clearly in love. Within twenty-four hours this was the front-page news on fifty-three papers around the world. Within royal circles it was referred to as "Black Wednesday."

### Diana's grandmother

Opposite: In July 1993 Lady Ruth
Fermoy, Diana's maternal
grandmother, passed away. She and
Charles attended the funeral at St.
Margaret's Church in King's Lynn. Lady
Fermoy had been one of the Queen
Mother's closest friends and served as
her lady-in-waiting for three decades.
Later that month Diana went to
Zimbabwe to visit projects run by three
different charities that she worked with:
the Red Cross, Help the Aged, and the
Leprosy Mission. Her visits included a
hospice for children suffering from
Aids and the Red Cross feeding center
at Masera, where she helped give out
food to waiting children.

Right: A kiss on the hand from a
member of the crowd at St. Matthew's
Community Centre at the Elephant and
Castle in South London. In November
photographs of Diana working out at
the LA Fitness Centre were published
in the *Sunday Mirror* and she took legal
action against the paper for invasion of
privacy. On December 3, during a
meeting for the Headway National
Head Injuries Association at the
Hilton, the Princess announced that
she was withdrawing from public life,
stating that she needed "time and
space" away from the attention of the
media. She said she would remain
patron of a few favorite charities but
would not accept any other
engagements until summer 1994.

## Away from official protection

Left: In April 1994 Diana's sister-in-law, Victoria, gave birth to a son, Louis Frederick. When the Princess arrived at St. Mary's Paddington to visit her new nephew, she had to pick her way through the waiting photographers. When Diana withdrew from public life she made the decision to give up any Royal protection unless she was with her sons. This did give her more freedom but also meant that she was under even more pressure from the media, which often led to outbursts and frustration at the invasion of her privacy.

Opposite: Diana had the opportunity to be reunited with Mother Teresa at the Missionaries of Charity in Kilburn, London. Making a special detour to England on her way from Washington to India, the nun had wanted to see Diana again. She admired the Princess's work and invited her to return to Calcutta to see the progress the missions had made.engagements until summer 1994.

## Police assistance

Opposite: Diana met friends William van Straubenzee, Kate Menzies, and Catherine Soames for lunch at San Lorenzo's. Unable to park and without any protection officers she had to resort to asking two Metropolitan Police officers to protect her car from traffic wardens; they put official memos under her windshield wipers and were later reprimanded for their actions.

Above: Diana took the boys to see the new ride "Nemesis" at Alton Towers; aghast at the sight of it she decided not to have a go, although William and Harry leapt at the chance.

## Dimbleby interview

Right: In a stunning off-the-shoulder cocktail dress designed by Christina Strombolian, Diana attended the *Vanity Fair* party at the Serpentine gallery. On the same evening a documentary about Prince Charles: "Charles: The Private Man, the Public Role", was screened on British television. Broadcaster Jonathan Dimbleby and a television crew had followed the prince for eighteen months and during the interview Charles admitted to adultery after his marriage to Diana had broken down. The following day in a press conference, the Prince's private secretary Richard Aylward named Camilla Parker Bowles as the other woman in his life.

Opposite: A radiant smile from the Princess brightens up a rainy day.

## Girl about town

Left and opposite: Diana could now enjoy the freedom of shopping in Kensington High Street, London. Despite her withdrawal from public life she had still attended the occasional official function for the charities she had selected, but toward the end of 1994 she started to gradually increase her workload. In October the follow-up book about Prince Charles, written by Jonathan Dimbleby, was serialized in the *Sunday Times*. The book gave more detail about his unhappy marriage. In the same month, cavalry officer James Hewitt published his memoirs announcing that he had a five-year affair with the Princess that began in 1986. He reportedly netted £1 million from his story.

## Camilla divorces

Opposite: An official engagement in January 1995 at the Royal Parks office in Hyde Park to present Royal Humane Society Awards to two men who rescued a tramp drowning in a lake in Regent's Park. Diana had been the first person to raise the alarm, seeing the incident during an early morning run. That month came the surprise announcement of the divorce of Camilla Parker Bowles and her husband Andrew. It was finalized in the decree absolute six weeks later.

Above: A train journey with William and a school friend to Cardiff to watch Ireland beat Wales 16–12 at Cardiff Arms Park.

### Resuming official duties

Opposite: In the spring of 1995 Diana made a brief visit to Venice before visiting Japan and Hong Kong. Before the Japanese tour she enlisted the help of writer Clive James, who taught her some Japanese phrases and loaned her his Japanese teacher. While there she formalized the link between Great Ormond Street Hospital for Sick Children and Tokyo's National Children's Hospital. Afterwards Diana made a very successful fund-raising trip to Hong Kong with millionaire David Tang, in one evening raising a quarter of a million pounds for various charities, including the Leprosy Mission in Hong Kong and China. She also traveled to Moscow where she was patron of a trust fund to improve the facilities at the Tushinskaya Children's Hospital in Moscow. In 1995 she was to attend 127 official engagements in total, compared to ten the previous year.

Left: A low-key outfit for a visit to the London Fashion Week.

### Help for the homeless

Opposite and left: Diana opened a hostel in June 1995 in Willesden, North London, run by the Depaul Trust. At the event, Cardinal Basil Hume paid tribute to Diana's work among the homeless and revealed that she would often make personal visits to hostels away from the media. As William and Harry grew up she would also take them along on occasions, to help them understand the lives of the less privileged. In July the family took part in what was to be their last official engagement together: at the 50th anniversary celebrations of VJ day in London, they sat together appearing very relaxed and happy.

### Following a family tradition

Opposite: William successfully passed his Common Entrance Examination and in September began his first term at Eton College. Diana had always wanted the boys to attend the school to follow the Spencer family tradition. The Prince and Princess and their two sons all arrived together, despite the ongoing divorce proceedings. On November 20 an interview between Diana and reporter Martin Bashir was screened by the BBC program *Panorama*. It had been recorded in secret at Kensington Palace and the Royal Family were only informed six days before the broadcast. Diana openly talked of her eating disorders and her relationship with James Hewitt. When questioned about her marriage she explained that it could never work as "there were three of us in this marriage." After the interview was broadcast Diana made an official statement that she agreed to Prince Charles's request for a divorce. Proceedings began immediately.

Left: Diana had been reunited with old friend Luciano Pavarotti when she flew into Italy. That summer she had taken William and Harry to America for a vacation, and while there they all rode horses in Colorado and went white-water rafting in Utah. Some of their stay was spent at Goldie Hawn's ranch in Aspen.

## Humanitarian award

Left: On December 12 Diana attended a lavish ceremony at the Hilton hotel, New York, where she was given the Humanitarian of the Year ward from the United Cerebral Palsy of New York Foundation. This honor, which she shared with General Colin Powell, was presented by Henry Kissinger and acknowledged her caring and compassionate achievements over the last fifteen years. Guests had paid £750 to attend the event and gave the Princess a standing ovation after her acceptance speech. While in New York Diana took the opportunity to return to the Harlem Children's Hospital that she had visited seven years earlier.

Opposite: Despite the disguise of dark glasses there were some days when Diana was continually harassed by the media. Photographs of the Princess would raise newspaper circulation figures and now that she was attending fewer official functions photographers needed to hunt her down to obtain the shots they needed. Meanwhile, the divorce proceedings between the Prince and Princes of Wales had progressed rapidly and with the final settlement agreed, a decree nisi was announced on July 15, 1996. In Court No.1 at Somerset House, their fifteen-year marriage was ended in little more than three minutes.

## Decree absolute

Opposite: Six weeks later, when the decree absolute came through, Diana was visiting the English National Ballet where crowds noticed she was still wearing her wedding and engagement rings. Under the terms of the divorce Diana received a lump sum payment of approximately £17 million, an annual allowance of £400,000 for her office and was allowed to keep her home at Kensington Palace. She lost the title "Her Royal Highness" but still retained the right to call herself Princess of Wales unless she remarried.

Right: A radiant smile as Diana attended a function in London. The previous September she had met surgeon Dr. Hasnat Khan when he operated on a friend at the Royal Marsden Hospital. A romance had begun, but they met in secret as Khan was a very private man averse to any publicity. In February Diana had traveled to Pakistan to meet his mother and had become very interested in Islam. In November, however, the news broke and the *Sunday Mirror* published a long article about their relationship.

### Focus on charity

Opposite and above: The Red Cross brought the landmines issue to Diana's attention. The charity was working to instigate a world-wide ban on the weapons and after watching a publicity film, the Princess felt she could contribute to its cause. In January 1997 Diana made her first visit to Angola on behalf of the Red Cross with director-general of the charity Mike Whitlam and Lord Deedes, a veteran landmine campaigner, who was representing the *Daily Telegraph*. It was estimated that there were 15 million mines throughout the country of 12 million inhabitants. Determined to bring the plight to the world's attention she worked with the Halo Trust, the mine clearance team, and very publicly walked through the middle of a half-cleared minefield in Cuito.

## Landmines in Luanda

Above: In Luanda Diana attended a mines awareness briefing session and learnt that there was one amputee for every 384 inhabitants. Arriving in the devastated town of Huambo she had to walk in single file behind an engineer to guarantee her safety. At the local hospital, which had very few medical supplies and only very basic facilities she met children and adults who had been maimed by stepping on mines. By the end of the eight-day tour, Diana's visit reached the headlines every day, which was exactly what she aimed to achieve.

Opposite: In March 1997 Charles and Diana were seen together in public for the first time since their divorce the previous year. The family attended William's confirmation at St. George's Chapel, Windsor. Their relationship had now improved and they were able to visit each other and attend the boys' school events together. At the end of June a charity sale of her dresses was held at Christies. Stemming from an idea from Prince William, eight hundred guests paid over £100 each to attend a preview party and the final sale of the dresses raised over $3 million with the majority going to the Aids Crisis Trust.

## Dodi Fayed

Left: In July Diana spent much of the month away but returned to London to open a new children's wing at Northwick Park hospital. Diana's relationship with Hasnat Khan had just ended and she had accepted an invitation from Mohamed Al Fayed to spend some time on his luxury yacht. There she met his son Dodi and a romance began instantly, with the couple dividing their time between London and France. However, the media soon started to harass them.

Opposite: Diana continued to promote the Red Cross landmines campaign with a brief visit to Bosnia in August. Two months earlier she had also flown to Washington to launch the American Red Cross anti-landmines campaign where in one gala evening alone $650,000 was successfully raised.

### Death of a Princess

Opposite: On Saturday August 31, after dining at the Ritz in Paris, Dodi and Diana were besieged by the paparazzi and the Mercedes they were traveling in crashed in the Alma tunnel. Dodi died instantly and Diana, although alive when she was cut free from the wreckage, died in hospital in the early hours of Sunday morning, after suffering a massive heart attack. There was an immediate outpouring of grief and within days a sea of flowers surrounded Kensington Palace, with people standing in line for hours to sign the book of condolence.

Above: On the day their mother died, William and Harry were at Balmoral and had the news broken to them by their father. At the funeral the following Saturday, Diana's bereft young sons walked silently behind their mother's coffin, flanked by Prince Charles, Prince Philip, and Earl Spencer.

### Farewell Diana

An estimated one million people poured into the capital to line the funeral procession route. At 9.08 the bells of Westminster began to toll and the gun carriage carrying Diana's coffin left Kensington Palace to travel to Westminster Abbey. Two thousand people attended her funeral service and afterwards, as the funeral cortège glided silently through the streets of London, members of the public bowed their heads and threw flowers at the hearse. The Princess of Wales then made the journey alone back to her family home in Northamptonshire, where she was buried on an island in the middle of a lake on the Althorp Estate.

Above: Diana won people's hearts across the world as she carved a role for herself, intent on "making a difference." She spent hours with those suffering from Aids or Leprosy, determined to drive out prejudice. Her charity work was phenomenal; as patron of over a hundred different organizations, she gave genuine support and compassion to those who needed it most. Diana left a joyous legacy in her beloved young sons; she raised William and Harry respecting Royal traditions, but prepared for the modern world. They have inherited her compassion and continued her charity work around the world.

## Acknowledgments

The photographs in this book are from the archives of Associated Newspapers. Particular thanks for the photographers' collective work over the last 30 years.

Thanks also to Steve Torrington, Alan Pinnock, Katie Lee, Dave Sheppard, Brian Jackson, Richard Jones and all the present staff.

Thanks also to Cliff Salter and John Dunne.